How to Build
WORLD PEACE
– IN –
Six Easy Steps
(and Posts)

...on the coming of a 21ˢᵗ Century America...

by P.R. Henika

How to Build World Peace in Six Easy Steps (and Posts)

ISBN 978-0-9971626-3-9

Printed in the United States of America

Second Edition

Published by:

Big Hat Press
Lafayette, California
www.bighatpress.com

For

Joseph, Carrie, Ava, Clara and Michael

ORIGIN

World Peace could begin as early as right now. The obvious and present choices of humanity are World War or World Peace. World Peace could start overnight. There is, however, very little talk and walk of World Peace in this day and age - anger seems prevalent. The World was tense prior to World War I. These pre-War tensions, not unlike the anger on display today, were unleashed as the ultimatums of World Wars I and II. The consequence of these World Wars was an unprecedented toll of human sacrifice - human sacrifice in the told millions. *A Culture of War*[a] was not born as much as it was justified: *Modern war itself is a culture - just as bureaucratic behavior is, or corporate behavior is, or the "herd instinct."*[a] And, those humans who did not want War chose against their wishes and better judgment and went to War anyway because they were sold, in part, on "necessity." Most people do not want war. There has even been a suggestion of "war weariness" - the recent opposition with regard to troops on the ground in Syria.

The precedents for World Peace could originate by consensus vote in seventeen days as did the United Nation's Resolution on counterterrorism measures - measures that were agreed upon by member nations after the shock and outrage that was the aftermath of 9/11:

> *On September 28, 2001, the Security Council was ready, without further discussion or debate, to adopt Resolution 1373, imposing, for the first time, an obligation on all countries to act across the board against terrorism and those providing material support for terrorism.*[b]

As I said above, World Peace could start overnight. The reality check posed for a putative rapid rise of World Peace is stated conclusively by John W. Dower: *Constructive change and deep cultures of peace will come, if at all, incrementally; and that is where the hope must reside.*[a] Perhaps resolve needs to replace hope.

So, if no one wants war then why does it happen? Sorry folks, I am not going to go on and on about how war is a *human invention*[c] designed to exploit - as an investment or as a profit motive for the military/oil complex. I am not going to dwell on how evil is also a human invention meant to exploit - about how some people use fear to sell media. I am not going to talk about how *groupthink*[a] or how *"top down and fractured communication"*[d] are probable administrative causes for the failure to protect America on 9/11. I want to know why most people do not want war and why the aversion to killing people and human kindness seem to be one of the reasons that a lot of people can go about their daily lives without being shot at or mugged. I want to know why all those shots were fired into the air - all those rounds wasted during World War II - all those rounds that were used to scare War away instead of confronting it in the way of the movies:

> *He* [Brigadier General Samuel L.A. Marshal] *found that only 15 to 20 percent of the veterans fired their weapons in combat, even when ordered to do so. Marshall concluded that most soldiers have a profound aversion to taking a life.*[c]

I want to know why World War seems to be the talk of the times and apparently, the preferred choice and commitment of the global leadership. I want to know why there is so little talk of World Peace or about how World Peace could be achieved. Is there a gene for the aversion to killing another human? Is there a gene for human kindness? I don't know.

I have heard - somewhere by someone - that the only thing anyone has to do is die. Sometimes, the probability of anyone's life span is simply a matter of one's birthplace. I should, no doubt, thank my lucky stars that I was born in America. Most of my life in

America has been a matter of choices and commitments - that was until the government was shut down last October 2014 and I was told that I could not go into my lab and do my research and that I wasn't going to be paid for the duration of the shutdown. In protest, I worked at home 24/7 until my lab was reopened. I was paid in full - don't know why. I was angry and shocked that I was living in America and that I was being told what I couldn't do without rhyme or reason. Still, the government shutdown was not death. I had the choice and the means to trespass into work. I complied and did not trespass.

Being told what to do are the precedents and practices of nations like North Korea - do or die there is not a matter of making or missing a free throw at a basketball game. There is little or no choice in North Korea. The choice to build World Peace is a *non-sequitur* in North Korea. The choice to build World Peace is a *non-sequitur* in America - the Land of the Free. What did you just say P.R. Henika? I said, between the lines, that there are two big picture scenarios that determine, in large part, the fate of humankind. It is quite possible that the 21st Century could be afflicted by World War III the latter of which could be accompanied with the continuation of a dependence on nonrenewable energy, the denial of the consequences of climate change and the denial of an increased rate of extinction. This is a perfectly valid big picture scenario for progress toward the collapse of, not just a single nation, but for most of human civilization. Honestly - it seems to be the scenario of choice - at least amongst the global leadership. Currently, it is still pretty much a worldwide *non-sequitur* but the other possibility for the 21st Century could be the human invention of World Peace the latter of which could be accompanied with a dependence, if you will, on renewable energy and sustainable development. It could also be accompanied by proactive adaptation such that the consequences of climate change are anticipated and the extinction rate is slowed down.

Many people love animals. Many people love dogs. Love is a

constant like the speed of light. The truth hurts that anyone's child or grandchild might miss out on 25% of the mammals by 2100 - that some species might be totally removed from their education:

> *It is estimated that one-third of all reef building corals, a third of all fresh water mollusks, a third of sharks and rays, a quarter of all mammals, a fifth of all reptiles and a sixth of all birds are headed for oblivion.*[e]

Some folks can't help themselves. Some folks hunt with a camera and the click of a mouse. So yes, I search for World Peace, not necessarily as appeasement or soft power, but as agreed-upon policies derived from 21st Century technology e.g. renewable energy and sustainable development.

RHETORIC

Humanity is at war with everything. There is thesis and antithesis. There is "us versus them." Bar none, a bold line can be drawn between war and peace. World Peace is the working hypothesis here. World War is the working null hypothesis here. The scientific method calls for responsibility - responsibility for the testing and evaluation of both the hypothesis and the null hypothesis. You know - try, evaluate, try again. The call for World War III is loud. The call for World Peace is merely a whisper. I even wonder sometimes if the mere mention of World Peace is taboo as though peace was only an accusation of altruism or that kind of pacifism that is assessed as defeatism e.g. giving in and rolling over to the demands of dictators. World Peace equates with appeasement and soft power for those who don't really want it. World Peace in the 21st Century equates with collaboration, compromise and consensus on issues that alleviate conflicts and benefit growth of the "better World" that is envisioned by many from citizens to Presidents. Like I said - humanity is at war with everything - at war with everything as evidenced by an omnipresent and unfortunate choice of specific descriptors and rhetoric. World Peace could begin overnight - by simply changing how global leaders describe policy.

The working hypothesis that is World Peace suggests that the *fight* against the consequences of climate change must end and that the adaptation to the consequences of climate change must begin. Proactive adaptation to climate change is currently not the favored rallying cry of many politicians. Humans seem receptive to the rally of national anthems, which, in many cases, glorify war. The daily peal at many sports events is a brief justification of a nation's confrontations. War, for some reason, excites humanity. There are the "wars" on terrorism and drugs, the "battle" against cancer, the "fight" for human rights, the onward righteous attacks of Christian soldiers etc. Even the likes of President Barak Obama and the United Nations refer to the policy of climate change as a "fight" or "combat":

> *That bright blue ball rising over the moon's surface, containing everything we hold dear – the laughter of children, a quiet sunrise, all the hopes and dreams of posterity – that's what's at stake. That's what we're fighting for. And if we remember that, I'm absolutely sure we'll succeed.* [f]
> - President Barack Obama, June 25, 2013

> *In this website you'll be able to find the latest news on what the UN is doing to combat climate change, information on the latest scientific reports, and successful initiatives that are already having a positive impact in society.* [g]

Humans seem highly motivated whenever they are in a fight for their lives or the quality of their lives. For years, I have written to the White House and Congress with the repeated suggestion that war rhetoric, in some cases, could be replaced with peacebuilding rhetoric as descriptors of policy. Peacebuilding, as a descriptor more frequently engaged, has gained some momentum in precedent but practice and funding are still minimal when compared to the "war chest." Again, I am not opposed to national anthems sung in remembrance but if the solution to climate change can be repeatedly described as proactive adaptation or as "ambitious action" [g] or if the solution to cancer can be repeatedly described as a cure or a healing then, as they say - "come what may."

RIGHTS

It has been thought of by the few, tested by the few and validated by the few but oh how slowly "it" - a paradigm shift - matures from precedent to practice. Humans now live in a newly proposed geological epoch called the Anthropocene[e] - a paradigm shift from the Holocene. This paradigm shift has already happened. The human impact on Earth has justified - not a Doomsday conspiracy - but a new geological epoch - a modern stratigraphy which, when looked upon in the future, may consist of the skeletal accomplishments of humanity and the bones of new species of rats simply because rats follow humans everywhere they go:[e]

> *Human activity has transformed between one third and one half of the land surface of the planet; most of the world's major rivers have been dammed or diverted; fertilizer plants produce more nitrogen than is fixed naturally by all terrestrial organisms; fisheries remove more than one third of the primary production of the ocean's coastal waters and humans use more than half of the world's readily available fresh water runoff.*[e]

The paradigm shift from World War to World Peace has not happened. In 1948, the United Nations voted by consensus that the 'right thing to do' after World War II *(a war to end all wars[h])* was to build a lasting World Peace for the first time in human history based on precedents and practices of the United Nation's Declaration of Universal Human Rights.[i] Everyone on the planet would conceivably be part of the goal and achievement that is World Peace - a World Peace based partly on the precedents and practices of human rights such that everyone would eventually be in working possession of all of their human rights.

How about a new future for America - a For the People future for America where the precedents and practices of a culture based on peacebuilding results in full employment for all Americans; a society where all Americans have all of their human rights working for them and - guess what - possibly little or no government because all American citizens just might discover, within *esprit de corps*, a conscientious responsibility for their choices, commitments and actions. Please do not confuse this scenario with Utopia or pacifism - problems will still be posed by Nature and other nations. Can we get there without sacrifice of freedom or security? Can we get there with the private and public sector working together? I think we can.

World Peace posits that humanity can choose peace over war. However, fundamental paradigm shifts need to happen:

> *I* [Jimmy Carter] *know that many people in Israel and abroad find it hard to accept the idea of talking to Hamas. The Elders utterly condemn any terrorist acts that harm innocent people. But if you're serious about peace-making, you have to sit down and talk to your enemies. It's what the British did in Northern Ireland, it's what the French did in Algeria, and it's what the Israelis themselves did with Yasser Arafat – someone once branded a terrorist who went on to win the Nobel Peace Prize together with Yitzhak Rabin.*[j]

It is obvious that World Peace did not happen after World War II. It was rudely pushed aside by MAD - the nonsensical *Mutually Assured Destruction*.[k] It was pushed aside by the human invention of the Cold War and by suspicions cultivated by the nuclear arms race. It was abandoned in part because of the American atrocities of Hiroshima and Nagasaki: "Peace, no peace," says the Extraterrestrial from Independence Day. We have had two World Wars but not one lasting World Peace.

DIPLOMACY

The number one security threat to humanity is climate change:

> *I've heard some folks try to dodge the evidence by saying they're not scientists; that we don't have enough information to act. Well, I'm not a scientist, either. But you know what – I know a lot of really good scientists at NASA, and NOAA, and at our major universities. The best scientists in the world are all telling us that our activities are changing the climate, and if we do not act forcefully, we'll continue to see rising oceans, longer, hotter heat waves, dangerous droughts and floods, and massive disruptions that can trigger greater migration, conflict, and hunger around the globe. The Pentagon says that climate change poses immediate risks to our national security. We should act like it.* [l]
> - President Barak Obama.

The big picture consequence of climate change in the 21st Century is also ominously combined with an accelerated rate of extinction - an extinction rate exacerbated by human activity - a Sixth Extinction [e] that could considerably shorten the legacy of humankind. Humans, of course, have the nuclear arsenal available for the destruction of humanity as another means of extinction. Humanity has the nuclear arsenal available for the destruction of the World not once but perhaps as much as three times over. [m] In the Middle East, the current major source of conflict is fresh water availability. Droughts in Syria have disenfranchised farmers and so they have migrated into suburbs and urban areas where they have become smugglers and recruits of anarchistic and terrorist groups:

> *"The drought did not cause Syria's civil war," said the Syrian economist Samir Aita, but, he added, the failure of the government*

to respond to the drought played a huge role in fueling the uprising. What happened, Aita explained, was that after Assad took over in 2000 he opened up the regulated agricultural sector in Syria for big farmers, many of them government cronies, to buy up land and drill as much water as they wanted, eventually severely diminishing the water table. This began driving small farmers off the land into towns, where they had to scrounge for work.[n]

Droughts have led to bread shortages in Egypt and hence the call for "aish" in Egypt's protests.[o] Yemen could be the first Middle Eastern nation to completely run out of fresh water.[p] Former President Jimmy Carter is currently in the Middle East and, as one of The Elders, he is calling for a revitalization of the election process in Palestine. President Carter, in the past, has emphasized the mutual respect and support of human rights by both Palestine and Israel as a requirement, as precedent and practice for a successful Middle East peace process:

The situation in Gaza is intolerable. Eight months after a devastating war, not one destroyed house has been rebuilt and people cannot live with the respect and dignity they deserve. Gaza's 1.8 million people are besieged, isolated and desperate. They cannot enjoy any of the aspects of normal life, from trade and travel to health and education, that people in my country – and indeed in Israel – take for granted.[j]

Setbacks in the Middle East peace process have been the result of the neglect and violation of human rights by one side or the other. The Middle East is considered by many to be the most volatile region in the World. The engagement of Middle East nations with nuclear weapons could conceivably ignite the flashpoint that is the beginning of the prophetic Antichrist War - a War that would put all of humanity in harm's way.

The hypothetical suggested here is, in short order, to define the current major source of conflict in the Middle East e.g. fresh water availability and to use diplomacy as a means to determine if fresh water can eventually be a sustainable resource for all the people of the Middle East such that all the people of the Middle East become part of the goals and achievements of human rights. The type of diplomacy posited here is called *tabula rasa* or clean slate diplomacy whereby diplomats refrain from historical precedent, preconceptions or preconditions and simply ask and answer questions about e.g. the availability of fresh water in the Middle East and what can be done via environmental planning to alleviate this source of conflict. Fortunately, Pope Francis has recently called for increased attention paid to and involvement of the Catholic Church with regard to the consequences of extinction and climate change the latter of which is, as stated above, the number one security threat in the World:

> *In the face of the emergencies of human-induced climate change, social exclusion, and extreme poverty, we join together to declare that: Human-induced climate change is a scientific reality, and its decisive mitigation is a moral and religious imperative for humanity. In this core moral space, the world's religions play a very vital role. These traditions all affirm the inherent dignity of every individual linked to the common good of all humanity(q) and the world should take note that the climate summit in Paris later this year (COP21) may be the last effective opportunity to negotiate arrangements that keep human-induced warming below 2-degrees C, and aim to stay well below 2-degree C for safety, and yet the current trajectory may well reach a devastating 4-degrees C or higher. Political leaders of all UN member states have a special responsibility to agree at COP21 to a bold climate agreement that confines global warming to a limit safe for humanity, while protecting the poor and the vulnerable from ongoing climate change that gravely endangers their lives.[q]*
> - Declaration of Religious Leaders, Political Leaders,

Business Leaders, Scientists and Development Practitioners - April 28, 2015

A 21ˢᵗ Century *tabula rasa* diplomacy would have President Trump reconsider the collaboration, compromise and consensus of Paris COP21 which posits that the reduction of greenhouse gases is the right course of action for all nations to take part.

PROSPERITY

Live long and prosper
- Spock

The Earth Statement[r] calls for deep decarbonization (a zero carbon society) by 2050:

> *In 2015, a good climate future is still within reach. If we act boldly, we can safeguard human development. It is a moral obligation, and in our self-interest, to achieve deep decarbonization of the global economy via equitable effort sharing. This requires reaching a zero-carbon society by mid-century or shortly thereafter, thereby limiting global warming to below 2°C as agreed by all nations in 2010. This trajectory is not one of economic pain, but of economic opportunity, progress and inclusiveness. It is a chance too good to be missed. We have just embarked upon a journey of innovation, which can create a new generation of jobs and industries, whilst enhancing the resilience of communities and people around the world.[r]*

The Earth Statement calls for eight elements of climate action to be taken before 2050 including: limit global warming to below 2C; leave 75% (not 100%) of fossil fuels in the ground; a phase out of greenhouse gases i.e. deep decarbonization; a phase in of a dependency, if you will, on renewable energy; a global agreement on deep decarbonization that is equitable; increased response i.e. collective action and scaled-up support for nations that are already experiencing the impact of climate change and the safeguard of carbon sinks such as forests, grasslands and aquatic systems. The eighth element addresses the finance of the response to and anticipation of the impact of climate change:

We must urgently realize new scales and sources of climate finance for developing countries to enable our rapid transition to zero-carbon, climate-resilient societies. This includes additional public funding for mitigation and adaptation at a level at least comparable to current global ODA [Official Development Assistance] (around 135 billion USD p.a.). Innovative schemes such as globally funded renewable energy feed-in tariffs are required. The private sector must be encouraged to mobilize substantially larger sums. Governments should engage with banks and pension funds, enabling a shift to climate-friendly investments. Global and national climate funding must be effective, transparent and accountable.[r]

The inequality of wealth distribution is without question an obstacle to the equality objectives of the UN's Declaration of Universal Human Rights the latter of which might say - *Live long and prosper* for everyone. How do we get to equal prosperity? Cooperative prosperity, in fits and starts, charts the course to equal prosperity and with it, economic strides toward an economy based on the precedents and practices of human rights. Along with it, cooperative prosperity or *conscious capitalism* may, for example, act as countermotivation to wannabe terrorists who might choose and commit to "family life." Peacebuilding becomes the new normal i.e. multiple paradigm shifts in synchrony toward a lasting World Peace.

The paradigm shift to World Peace could happen in a very short time with nations on the same page – a United Nation's Resolution for the end of war rhetoric; the respect and support of human rights; the engagement of tabula rasa diplomacy and the call for conscious capitalism. A prosperity that includes profit and salary sharing, full employment, the investment of the private and public sector in renewable energy and sustainable development could all occur rather quickly. The exaggerations that are World War III, complete denials of climate change and complete denials of extinction bode ill - that synergy which shortens the legacy of humankind and charters a dark future for our children and grandchildren. As I recall, President Obama has described the big picture as a ship moving slowly forward - the course of which is difficult to change but what if we were to unload the cargo of War and replace it with the cargo of Peace. I prefer Resolution to the alterative expressed in the movie *Star Trek - The Voyage Home*:

> *It is difficult to answer when one does not understand the question. Mister President, perhaps you should transmit a planet distress signal - while we still have time.*[s]
> - Sarek

URGENCY

There exists a nation on Earth that is almost totally in the dark. Satellite images of North Korea clearly show that: *South Korea is filled with lights and energy and vitality and a booming economy; North Korea is dark.*[t] North Korea is isolated. Frankly, I never thought that complete isolation of a nation was possible in a World that is coming closer and closer together via such inventions as the Worldwide Web. Isolation favors the World War III paradigm. Isolation works to slow the paradigm shift to World Peace. Some nation's manifestos call for isolation: *He* [President Vladimir Putin] *said that foreign interference in Russian affairs should not be allowed, that Russia has its own free will.*[u] Others call for urgency:

> *We urgently need to change course and catalyze a transformation of the way we develop, the way we live and the way we do business. Our current system is flawed and unsustainable and if it continues the world is on course for catastrophic climate change and vast inequality.*[v]
> - Mary Robinson, April 22, 2015

> *A new global citizens' movement is heeding the scientific evidence, demanding immediate climate action. Societies across the world have given political leaders a mandate and a responsibility to act for a safe climate future now. Informed by scientific knowledge, inspired by economic assessments and guided by the moral imperative, we call on world leaders to work towards the following eight essential elements* [listed above] *of a Paris Agreement and associated set of actions and plans that would represent a global turning point in December 2015.*[r]
> - The Earth Statement

UNITED NATIONS RESOLUTION PROPOSAL

Recent studies have demonstrated that ocean acidification was responsible for the last phase Permian extinction event, which took ~60,000 years to extinguish 90% of the World's species. Now the human achievement of The Sixth Extinction (Pulitzer winning book) is moving at a much more rapid rate. Wow - the Human legacy - extinction in record time. It is time to end the prospect of World War III and a dependence on nonrenewable energy. It is time to make the tectonic shift to building World Peace and a dependence on renewable energy and sustainable development. The multilateral way to World Peace is via United Nation's Resolution with nations voting based on collaboration, compromise and consensus. I probably sound like a broken record by now but I think World Peace can be built without concession, without loss of security and without sacrifice of freedom.

The call here is for a comprehensive and pragmatic World Peace via this proposed UN Resolution: (1) end of war rhetoric/solutions and replacement with peacebuilding rhetoric/solutions i.e. the solution to climate change is not, according to the U.N. and President Obama, a "fight" or "combat" - it is proactive adaptation; (2) respect and support of human rights as goals and achievements - the realization of the U.N.'s Declaration of Universal Human Rights of 1948 and the U.N.'s Sustainable Development Plan of 2015; (3) *tabula rasa* diplomacy - diplomacy without historical precedent, preconceptions or preconditions; (4) conscious capitalism - profit and salary sharing; full employment; renewable energy jobs and markets etc.; (5) conversion of military to responders to natural disasters - those natural disasters posed by climate change and (6) conversion of intelligence agencies to account for the efficient use of foreign aid.

REFERENCES

(a) *Cultures of War: Pearl Harbor, Hiroshima, 9/11, Iraq*, John W. Dower, W.W. Norton and Company, New York and London, 2010, page 437, page 452.

(b) *Flawed Diplomacy: The United Nations and the War on Terrorism*, Victor D. Comras, Potomac Books Inc., Washington D.C., 2010, page 77.

(c) *The End of War*, John Horgan, McSweeney's Books, San Francisco, 2012. Pages 142-143.

Quote: *Like Margaret Mead,* [John] *Mueller views war as a cultural "idea" or "invention" that has gripped humanity for millennia. War is "an institution" he writes, "that has been grafted onto human existence, rather than a trick of fate, a thunderbolt from hell, a natural calamity, a systemic necessity, or a desperate plot dreamed up by some sadistic puppeteer on high.* He disagrees with Mead only on the point that we need to invent something to replace war. The advocacy in this book includes the human invention of World Peace as a replacement for World War III.

Note: Page 57 - Marshall polled 400 companics of infantrymen who fought in Europe and the Pacific.

(d) "Who's out of the loop?" Dr. Charles M. Kelly, *The Charlotte Observer*, April 11, 2004, http://www.kellysite.net/obsloop.htm.

Note: The author does not actually use the phrase 'top down fractured communication.' The latter is an interpretation of problems of *upward and cross-unit communication.*

(e) *The Sixth Extinction: An Unnatural History*, Elizabeth Kolbert, Henry Holt and Company, New York, 2014, pages 17-18, page 108.

(f) https://www.whitehouse.gov/energy

(g) http://www.un.org/climatechange/

(h) Note: Actually, the phrase originated in reference to World War I http://en.wikipedia.org/wiki/The_war_to_end_war - "The war to end war" (sometimes called "The war to end all wars")[1] was a term for World War I. Originally idealistic, it is now used mainly in a disparaging way.[2] *The War to End All Wars*, BBC News, November 10, 1998,[1] *Safire's Political Dictionary*, William Safire, 2008.[2]

(i) http://www.un.org/en/documents/udhr/

(j) "The situation in Gaza is intolerable": Why a paradigm shift is needed in Israel and Palestine, email from Jimmy Carter - http://theelders.org, received May 8, 2015.

(k) http://en.wikipedia.org/wiki/Mutual_assured_destruction

Note: Mutually Assured Destruction (MAD), is a doctrine of military strategy and national security policy in which a full-scale use of high-yield weapons of mass destruction by two or more opposing sides would cause the complete annihilation of both the attacker and the defender.

(l) "President calls climate change the 'greatest threat to future generations' in State of the Union," Rebecca Jacobsen, January 21, 2015.
http://www.pbs.org/newshour/updates/president-calls-climate-change-greatest-threat-future-generations-state-union/

Quote: *No challenge poses a greater threat to future generations than climate change,"* Mr. Obama said. *"2014 was the planet's warmest year on record. Now, one year doesn't make a trend, but this does - 14 of the 15 warmest years on record have all fallen in the first 15 years of this century.*

(m) This comment is subject to debate: http://en.wikipedia.org/wiki/Nuclear_holocaust - The belief in "overkill" is also commonly encountered, with an example being the following statement made by nuclear disarmament activist Philip Noel-Baker in 1971 - *Both the US and the Soviet Union now possess nuclear stockpiles large enough to exterminate mankind three or four - some say ten - times over*, with Brian Martin suggesting that the origin of this belief is from *crude linear extrapolations*, and when it is analyzed it has no basis in reality.[10] "The global health effects of nuclear war," Brian Martin, *Current Affairs Bulletin*, 59(7), pages 14-26, December, 1982.
http://www.bmartin.cc/pubs/82cab/

(n) "Without Water, Revolution," Thomas L. Friedman, *New York Times*, May 18, 2013 and see Showtime's *Years of Living Dangerously*, http://yearsoflivingdangerously.com

(o) "Bread Is Life: Food and Protest in Egypt," Krista Mahr, *Time*, January 31, 2011.

Quote: *If the* [wheat] *import doesn't materialize, I don't think Egypt has enough supplies domestically to meet the demands of the population," says* [FAO senior economist Abdolreza] *Abbassian. "There is a sense of insecurity in the city. The last thing you want is the subsidy to start failing." If that happens, the demonstrations that have been chiefly political in nature may very well take a sharp and potentially dangerous turn, and the government could have a new kind of emergency on its hands. "Whoever takes over knows that meeting the food demand of the 80 million will be the highest priority," says Abbassian. "I don't think there could be any bigger priority than this.*

(p) "What If Yemen Is the First Country to Run Out of Water?" Krista Mahr, *Time*, December 14, 2010.

Quote: *The water shortage is also a global problem, because, like Somalia across the Gulf of Aden, where desertification has been linked with that county's ongoing conflict, fights and desperation over water in Yemen would be exactly the kind of destabilizing factor that insurgents will need to continue to strengthen their base in remote areas far from the halls of power.*

(q) Vatican summit: 'There is a moral imperative to act on climate change', *Catholic Herald*, April 29, 2015.
http://www.catholicherald.co.uk/news/2015/04/29/vatican-summit-there-is-a-moral-imperative-to-act-on-climate-change/

(r) *Earth Statement*, April 22, 2015 (Earth Day)
http://earthstatement.org/statement/

(s) http://www.chakoteya.net/movies/movie4.html

(t) http://www.globalsecurity.org/military/world/dprk/dprk-dark.htm

(u) http://en.wikipedia.org/wiki/Russian_presidential_election,_2012

(v) "Climate justice: why is it relevant in 2015?" Mary Robinson, April 22, 2015.
http://theelders.org/article/climate-justice-why-it-relevant-2015
See also Mary Robinson Foundation of Climate Justice
http://www.mrfcj.org

Note: *We haven't yet created this social and international order – and any hope of creating it in the future would be wiped out by uncontrolled climate change. But I think we could create an international order where all people realise their rights if we grasp the opportunities 2015 presents.*
Now is not the moment to manage expectations or get cold feet – 2015 is

the moment to catalyse a transformation – and achieve the social order the *Universal Declaration* [of Human Rights] *aspired to. Now is the time for climate justice.* - Mary Robinson

POSTS

...on the coming of a 21st Century progressive America...

September 11, 2017

The Will to Move On from 9/11 - The cost of 9/11, IMO, is the pervasive 'us versus them' i.e. the division in America that 9/11 caused and the acceptance of that division as the new normal. The acceptance of 'us versus them' as the new normal has kept America stuck in the past i.e. America has not moved past the 20th Century in terms of leadership and governance. But there are recent signs that that could change i.e. angry Americans might just take pause and start to search for 21st Century solutions. Oddly enough Donald Trump might accidentally be the sign of such movement forward simply by his willingness to dialogue and work with "Chuck" and "Nancy." The willingness of currently intransigent conservatives like Mitch McConnell to work in bipartisan fashion with Democrats on e.g. ACA fixes just might be the next revelation. It could be that Trump is tired of being hated and that he seeks success in a way that includes working with Democrats. There are progressive Republicans amongst us who are willing and able to lead America into the 21st Century. Republican Will Hurd has bipartisan support for a SMART Wall that is cost effective and employs 21st Century technology. George Bush talks about points of light - a light coming on here and there - and so where is the will to move toward those lights from the shadows created by 9/11?

September 8, 2017

When is Trump et al going to start working in a bipartisan fashion to help move America into the 21st Century? In the 21st Century, the

SMART Wall is built instead of Trump's Wall. In the 21st Century, Citi Stat addresses all crime not just immigrant crime. In the 21st Century, the UN's Sustainable Development Plan succeeds such that all nations emerge from poverty and into prosperity. In the 21st Century, humans have all their human rights working for them. In the 21st Century, the militaries of the World become the first responders to climate change i.e. they save lives instead of killing people. In the 21st Century, nations cooperate to reduce greenhouses. Finally, 21st Century diplomacy offers help for nations to help themselves and the dialogue can be offered without concession, without appeasement and without compromise. World War III could happen simply because of what some of the global leadership including Trump and Putin didn't want to talk about e.g. renewable energy.

August 24, 2017

Bipartisanship is getting things done. Examples include (1) sanctions against Russia and North Korea, (2) Rapid DNA Act of 2017 re: DNA analysis i.e. DNA profiles in 90 minutes, (3) proposals for ACA fixes and (4) proposals for protection of Special Counsel Mueller's Russia investigation. America and the rest of the World is moving into the 21st Century with bipartisan support for single payer health insurance, for adaptation to climate change (it was thought nations might follow Trump's sign-off of Paris COP21 - they haven't), for green jobs and green markets, for sustainability, for prosperity etc. America and the rest of the World is moving into the 21st Century in spite of Trump i.e. Trump is the one in isolation not the rest of America and the World. When will Mitch McConnell and the like go bipartisan?

August 22, 2017

Afghanistan - The war in Afghanistan has gone on too long. The people of Afghanistan are expected to rebuild in the ruins of war and without the professionals required as professionals are the first to leave as refugees. The people of Afghanistan are expected to forget the innocents killed and their families torn apart. The people of Afghanistan are expected to step aside for America's declared mineral rights or for America's Blackwater mercenaries who exploit security for profit. The people of Afghanistan are expected to rebuild and restore their culture without help from America - America bombs, kills and then they leave. "No nation building," says Trump washing his hands of any responsibility and talking as if nation building had actually been tried and tested. It hasn't. A 21st Century foreign policy includes establishment of safe zones and then the insertion of peace building forces to help with the restoration of Afghanistan culture and, if they chose, the benefits of 21st Century technology. In Africa, a single solar panel can power a light bulb and that light bulb means an education. There is no such thing as a "win" in Afghanistan. Military intervention only ensures failed states.

August 21, 2017

Bipartisanship News - "IntegenX Inc., the global market leader for Rapid DNA human identification, applauds the signing into law of S.139 and HR.510, The Rapid DNA Act of 2017. The legislation will allow law enforcement agencies, under standards and guidelines established by the FBI, to perform real-time DNA testing at time of arrest, within booking stations. Similar to how fingerprint analysis has evolved from a paper and ink practice to a point-of-action technology, DNA testing has now become possible in 90 minutes within a booking station, while a suspect is still in custody. With processing times reduced from weeks to less than two hours, the potential to identify or exonerate a suspect quickly will make a meaningful impact on law enforcement. IntegenX thanks U.S. Senate sponsor Senator Orrin Hatch (R-UT) and lead co-sponsor Senator Dianne Feinstein (D-CA) as well as House sponsor Congressman James Sensenbrenner (R-WI) and lead co-sponsor Congressman Eric Swalwell (D-CA), along with the other 12 Senate and 24 House co-sponsors for their support."

"IntegenX Applauds the Passage of the Rapid DNA Act of 2017"; *Business Wire*; August 21, 2017

https://finance.yahoo.com/news/integenx-applauds-passage-rapid-dna-120000371.html

August 20, 2017

Eight Snowflakes (originally Seven Snowflakes) -

*Snowflake #1 - Renewable energy e.g. green jobs and green markets.

*Snowflake #2 - Prosperity for all nations and immigration by choice.

*Snowflake #3 - Sustainable development e.g. the 17 goals of the UN's Sustainable Development Plan of 2015.

*Snowflake #4 - Inclusive politics e.g. bipartisanship and global cooperatives such as the Trans Pacific Partnership and the Paris COP21.

*Snowflake #5 - Adaptation to climate change i.e. environmental impact studies that include climate change models.

*Snowflake #6 - Community i.e. the reduction of all crime not just immigrant crime e.g the administration of Citi Stat.

*Snowflake #7 - Human Rights - all of everyone's human rights

working for them i.e. all lives matter and all citizens take responsibility for their actions.

*Snowflake #8 - Oooppps - Forgot Universal Health Care

America has nothing to lose with the declaration of these snowflakes and everything to gain in terms of moving America into the 21st Century.

August 19, 2017

Congressman Eric Swalwell's precedents and practices are steeped in bipartisanship which begins with recognition of argument flaws on both sides of the aisle. Congressman Eric Swalwell's precedents and practices are also steeped in 21st Century resources and innovation. Congressman Eric Swalwell has consistently invited Republicans to the same table - sometimes they came e.g. Ebola; sometimes they didn't e.g. gun ownership responsibility and sometimes they ignored e.g. a bipartisan independent investigation re: the Russia investigation. I agree with Trump re: his call for "unity." I am an advocate of bipartisanship so I agree with Trump that both sides have flawed arguments e.g. the right's authoritarianism and the left's righteous indignation. I have singled you out as a simple matter of point/counterpoint. Finally, I reserve praise for the truth told in detail and for the solution served for the benefit of all Americans. Trump has not, in any way, measured up to this standard. Congressman Eric Swalwell has measured up to this standard in a contemporary and innovative way e.g. Future Forum. Nope, no praise for Trump until he chooses to work with Democrats in a bipartisan fashion.

August 19, 2017

Congressional bipartisanship is the means by which unity is

achieved and big problems can be solved with the application of 21st Century resources and innovation. A bipartisan investigation of domestic terrorism resides in the House Homeland Security Committee with Texas Republican Michael McCaul as chair. Congressman Eric Swalwell has served on this Committee re: a bipartisan address of the Ebola epidemic. There have been numerous internal "wars" declared recently or revived - Bannon/Breitbart vs the globalists, Trump versus the Democrats, Trump trolls vs. the liberals, alt-right vs. the Establishment, Trump vs. North Korea, Trump vs Venezuela, Trump versus the Taliban, Trump vs. ISIS, Neo Nazis vs. the Establishment, the KKK versus the Establishment, the left vs. Confederate statues, Antifa against the alt-right... Yes, there are flawed arguments on both sides - the authoritarianism of the right and the righteous indignation of the left. The talk of war is becoming inexorable - the roars of many mice. There needs to be a bipartisan and independent investigation by the House Homeland Security Committee re: domestic terrorism and the sooner the better.

August 18, 2017

America's Newest Enemy - The Bannon/Breitbart declared war will undoubtedly use staged controversy as its weapon and will undoubtedly incite more domestic terrorism. The Bannon/Breitbart declared war has already invented an enemy - the "globalists." The alt right and the "alt left" were recognized as present at Charlottesville but the globalists were not mentioned. The globalists were not present at Charlottesville because Bannon/Breitbart hadn't engaged them yet. So, what is the poison that dissolves the Bannon/Breitbart declared war and sends them back into the hole from which they came? The poison is bipartisanship i.e. this simple and practical idea that Democrats and Republicans can work together to solve problems and that they can solve big problems using 21st Century resources and innovation. Bipartisanship is the weapon that America can use to counter Bannon/Breitbart. The source of this bipartisanship is based on the succession of power ceded to Congress in the Constitution where Congress is America's first and foremost deliberative and legislative body and not Bannon/Breitbart or the Neo Nazi's or Donald Trump.

August 18, 2017

There is only a 1/22 million chance of being killed by an Islamist terrorist in America since 9/11 and the incidents of Islamic terrorism in America are the lowest in the World. The reasons for this stellar stat are intelligence gathering, law enforcement and a Muslim American community who teaches that Islam is a peaceful religion as agreed to by many Republicans e.g. George Bush. Trump seems to have a problem with the facts: "Trump said that Pershing stopped 'radical Islamic terror' for 35 years. Of the eight historians we checked with the first time we heard Trump speak about Pershing, all were at least skeptical that the specific tales of Pershing actually took place, and some expressed disbelief even more forcefully than that. But more critically, the historians took issue with Trump's suggestion that the tactic - if it was even used at all - actually worked to end tensions, noting that unrest persisted for years. Trump's claim rates Pants on Fire."

"Donald Trump retells Pants on Fire claim about Gen. Pershing ending terrorism for 35 years"; by Louis Jacobson, Aaron Sharockman on Thursday, August 17, 2017

http://www.politifact.com/truth-o-meter/statements/2017/aug/17/donald-trump/donald-trump-retells-pants-fire-claim-about-gen-pe/

August 17, 2017

A win for diversity - It was a strange moment of triumph against racism: The gun-slinging white supremacist Craig Cobb, dressed up for daytime TV in a dark suit and red tie, hearing that his DNA testing revealed his ancestry to be only "86 percent European, and … 14 percent Sub-Saharan African." The studio audience whooped and laughed and cheered. And Cobb - who was, in 2013, charged with terrorizing people while trying to create an all-white enclave in North Dakota - reacted like a sore loser in the schoolyard.

"Wait a minute, wait a minute, hold on, just wait a minute," he said, trying to put on an all-knowing smile. "This is called statistical noise."

See - "White Nationalists Are Flocking to Genetic Ancestry Tests - with Surprising Results; Sometimes they find they are not as 'white' as they'd hoped"; By Eric Boodman, August 16, *Scientific American*

https://www.scientificamerican.com/article/white-nationalists-are-flocking-to-genetic-ancestry-tests-with-surprising-results/

August 16, 2017

Bipartisanship News - (1) Censure -"Three Democrats on Wednesday announced plans to introduce a House resolution censuring Trump for his remarks, which included the suggestion made Tuesday that some 'very fine people' were among those who participated in the racist 'Unite the Right' march and that 'both sides' were to blame for violence that killed a Charlottesville woman and injured many others." Censure will take a House vote and will be a test as to how Republicans align with or distance themselves from Trump. (2) "There was one sign of bipartisan cooperation Wednesday — though one not aimed directly at Trump. The House Homeland Security Committee said a hearing next month on terrorist threats would include a discussion of racist extremism, following a demand from the panel's Democrats for a public examination of the white nationalist movement." As far as I can tell, the media has been mostly critical of what they consider a lack of action by of Congress. However, I still think that bipartisan efforts are worth the recognition and the details such as scrutiny of Homeland Security Committee and its hearing next month on domestic terrorism.

House Democrats push GOP to do more than talk tough on Trump.

https://www.washingtonpost.com/powerpost/house-democrats-push-gop-to-do-more-than-talk-tough-on-trump/2017/08/16/b947dc3e-82aa-11e7-b359-15a3617c767b_story.html?utm_term=.860762a51f9a

August 15, 2017

"Democrats on the House Homeland Security Committee are asking panel Chairman Michael McCaul (R-Texas) to examine racist fringe groups, including those that organized Saturday's violent protest against the removal of a statue of Confederate Gen. Robert E. Lee on the University of Virginia campus."

California Rep. Lou Correa, who sits on the Homeland panel, was the first Democrat to call for hearings. "Yesterday's horrific acts against innocent Americans were clear acts of terrorism," he said. "Our country has a homegrown terrorism problem we refuse to address. That ends now. We must hold hearings and finally address that terrorism inflicted by white supremacy extremists is destroying our country."

Dems demand scrutiny of white supremacists and domestic terrorism.

http://www.msnbc.com/rachel-maddow-show/dems-demand-scrutiny-white-supremacists-and-domestic-terrorism?cid=sm_fb_maddow

August 14, 2017

It is over: "They have been condemned" - Donald Trump - except perhaps for the rallies scheduled in nine cities this weekend (including Mountain View, CA): "The events scheduled for this coming Saturday—a 'free speech' rally in Boston and marches scheduled in nine cities to protest Google's firing of an employee who wrote a screed against diversity—will help clarify where all the chaotic elements that comprise the alt-right are headed in the near-term future. (The anti-Google protests are slated for Atlanta, Los Angeles, Pittsburgh, Seattle, New York, Washington, Austin, Boston, and Mountain View, California. On Sunday, organizers released a statement condemning violence and insisting that they are 'in no way associated with any group who organized' in Charlottesville.)"

See - "What the Next Round of Alt-Right Rallies Will Reveal; Protests scheduled in nine American cities for Saturday will provide a sense of where the movement is headed"; J.M. Berger; *The Atlantic*; August 14, 2017

https://www.theatlantic.com/politics/archive/2017/08/the-alt-right-stands-at-a-crossroads/536748/

August 14, 2017

The Democrats offer America bipartisanship, universal health care, adaptation to climate change, jobs, global cooperatives, renewable energy, inclusive politics, data-driven government and human rights. What does Trump et al have to offer America?

See - "President Trump just can't bring himself to unequivocally condemn and repudiate white supremacy and its modern-day equivalent, the 'alt-right.'"

https://www.splcenter.org/news/2017/08/13/stand-now-mr-president

August 13, 2017

Blame from "both sides"? Seriously? White supremacist motivated attacks from the Trump et al side are responsible for the current violence and so does Charlottesville's mayor agree: "'Look at the campaign he ran,' Charlottesville Mayor Michael Signer said in an interview with CNN's State of the Union on Sunday. 'I mean, look at the intentional courting, both on the one hand of all these white supremacists, white nationalists - a group like that - anti-Semitic groups, and then look on the other hand the repeated failure to step up, condemn, denounce, silence, you know, put to bed all those different efforts, just like we saw yesterday. I mean, this is not hard.'"

See - "Charlottesville mayor largely blames Trump for white supremacist violence"; Dylan Stableford; Senior Editor; *Yahoo News*; August 13, 2017

https://www.yahoo.com/news/charlottesville-mayor-largely-blames-trump-white-supremacist-violence-175055166.html

August 12, 2017

"Our report found that the campaign is producing an alarming level of fear and anxiety among children of color and inflaming racial and ethnic tensions in the classroom. Many students worry about being deported."

"The Trump Effect: The Impact of the Presidential Campaign on Our Nation's Schools"; April 13, 2016; SPLC

https://www.splcenter.org/20160413/trump-effect-impact-presidential-campaign-our-nations-schools

August 11, 2017

Twenty-first Century Diplomacy - Three possibilities - (1) Renewable energy is 21st Century diplomacy. Why? Nonrenewable sources are located in quantity in only specific nations. Nonrenewable sources are a source of conflict. The Sun belongs to no one and thus renewable energy is not a subject of conflict and it has the potential for global cooperatives as a matter of 21st Century diplomacy. Let us talk to North Korea about renewable energy. (2) Adaptation to climate change could benefit from the end of war. Twenty-first Century diplomacy calls for the end of war but for the keeping of the World's militaries. Why? Militaries in the 21st Century could be used as first responders and engineers to the challenges presented by climate change. Let us talk to North Korea about ending war and using the military to save lives instead of killing people and (3) Twenty-first Century diplomacy is the application of big data to solution of big problems. We live in the information age derived from data mining. In other words, the answers for any specific problem may already have been stored. If not, multivariate statistics allows for shorter time tables re: scientific investigations. Let's talk to North Korea about the human face of big data. For sure, 21st Century diplomacy is not appeasement nor is it soft power.

August 9, 2017

Yes, it is true that the only thing Trump understands is strength. What Trump does not understand is that diplomacy is strength as well e.g. the cease fire on the Korean Peninsula has been in place since the 1950's due, in part, to diplomacy. What is the required now is a diplomatic effort that helps move North Korea into the 21st Century. I have described that kind of diplomacy as diplomacy without preconditions, preconceptions and historical precedent. Tillerson is not offering this kind of diplomacy but Dianne Feinstein is offering diplomacy without preconditions. The second kind of effort is containment and defense e.g. ballistic missile defense systems (see link below). Trump does not seem to recognize advances in diplomacy as global cooperatives nor does he seem to recognize the technological advances re: containment and defense. Trump is not using all resources available to him nor is he presenting a complete picture to the American people on how America could respond to the threat by North Korea. Rhetoric re: America's diplomatic strength and containment/defense strength should precede the military option as an assurance to the people of Guam, South Korean and Japan - those people who Trump so impulsively and casually put into harm's way.

https://fas.org/wp-content/uploads/media/Nuclear-Dynamics-In-A-Multipolar-Strategic-Ballistic-Missile-Defense-World.pdf

August 9, 2017

Re: North Korea - Diplomacy has worked since the cease fire in the 1950s. Diplomacy has not advanced the cease fire to a peace accord which is the next step. The type of diplomacy that has not been tested is a diplomacy without preconditions as recommended by Dianne Feinstein. Trump has exercised the military option only and the military option that normalizes the use of nuclear weapons which puts the people of Guam, South Korea and Japan in harm's way. By ignoring containment and tabula rasa or clean slate diplomacy, Trump has failed to use all resources available to him. The goal of diplomacy in the 21st Century is to help nations move into a 21st Century progressive environment and so this another option available to North Korea - an option that Trump has not considered.

August 8, 2017

Authoritarians like Trump like it simple, powerful and punitive. The three options for response to North Korea are: (1) containment, (2) diplomacy and (3) military. Trump has not mentioned containment or diplomacy but today, in keeping with his authoritarian modus operandi, he threatened North Korea with the military option e.g. the preemptive strike. Trump just put millions of South Korean and Japanese in the line of fire either wittingly or unwittingly. My guess is that it is unwittingly and that the rhetoric was guided, not by the advice of his Generals, but by his own temperament - a temperament predicted correctly during the campaign as being unfit for Commander-in-Chief.

August 8, 2017

State controlled media? Trump Administration doubles down on the growth of Russian propaganda in the U.S. in order to keep Putin happy (1,2): (1) Secretary of State Tillerson seeks to deny funding for countering Russian propaganda in the US and (2) Sinclair will be in 72% of American homes that would "far exceed the federal limit on media ownership."

(1) "Secretary of State Rex Tillerson is resisting the pleas of State Department officials to spend nearly $80 million allocated by Congress for fighting terrorist propaganda and Russian disinformation."

"Trump's State Department finds new ways to make Russia happy"; by Steve Benen; August 2, 2017 http://www.msnbc.com/rachel-maddow-show/trumps-state-deptartment-finds-new-ways-make-russia-happy

(2) "In May, the Maryland-based Sinclair announced its $3.9 billion purchase of Tribune Media Co., which would expand its reach to major markets including New York, Los Angeles, and Chicago. The deal, Politico's Margaret Harding McGill and John Hendel report, would not be possible if not for a decision by Republican FCC Chairman Ajit Pai to revive a decades-old regulatory loophole that will keep Sinclair from vastly exceeding federal limits on media ownership. By adding 42 Tribune stations to the 173 it already owns, Sinclair will be in 72 percent of American homes, a number that would far exceed the federal limit on media ownership if not for Pai's action."

"Concerns, political and commercial, over Sinclair's dominance of local TV"; by Pete Vernon, *CJR*; August 8, 2017

https://www.cjr.org/analysis/concerns-political-and-commercial-over-sinclairs-dominance-of-local-tv.php

August 6, 2017

Currently - "California (199,038 GWh) is currently the 4th largest renewable energy producer in the United States behind Pennsylvania (214,811 GWh), Florida (238,094 GWh), and Texas (455,532 GWh). By percent, California is the 8th highest in percent renewable energy, while Texas produces over double the amount of renewable energy as California. Given California's significant energy consumption they will likely need assistance from states like Texas in building systems large enough to supply consistent renewable energy to the state."

"Both California and Texas fully recognize the energy transition

37

yet appear to be motivated differently. California is motivated by a cleaner environment and lessening the impacts of climate change. Whereas Texas is motivated capitalistically in seeing renewable energy and the energy transition as an economic opportunity."

"California Goes All In - 100% Renewable Energy 2045"; by Trevor Nace; August 1, 2017

https://www.forbes.com/sites/trevornace/2017/08/01/california-goes-all-in-100-percent-renewable-energy-by-2045/

August 4, 2017

Here is another example of bipartisanship i.e. blocking of the Trump et al putative agenda - no Trump appointments during the Congressional recess by consensus vote of all 100 Senators This joins the Senate bipartisan vote to issue sanctions on Russia and support President Obama's expulsion of Russian diplomats and seizure of Russian dachas based on Putin sanctioned hacking of our election. There is bipartisan agreement that intelligence gathered and presented to President Obama in August 2016 is proof of Putin sanctioned interference in our electoral process. There is bipartisan support for Special Counsel's Robert Mueller's independence into the Russia investigation. There are two bipartisan bills introduced by Republican Tillis and Democrat Coons and Republican Graham and Democrat Booker that would make it difficult for Trump to remove Special Counsel Mueller. There was bipartisan support for Jeff Sessions. There have been some statements by Republicans Murkowski and Collins that, with regard to health care, representation of their constituents take precedent over loyalty to Trump. There has been bipartisan dialogue on ACA fixes. None of this bipartisanship has been the result of fake news or leaks.

"Senators head home, and block Trump recess appointments";
AFP Michael Mathes; AFP; August 3, 2017

https://www.yahoo.com/news/senators-head-home-block-trump-recess-appointments-020513769.html

August 3, 2017

More bipartisanship in the Senate re: protection of Robert Mueller from Trump et al and assurance of independence for the Special Counsel investigation.

"One plan by Sens. Thom Tillis, R-N.C., and Chris Coons, D-Del., would let any special counsel for the Department of Justice challenge his or her removal in court. A three-judge panel would review the dismissal within 14 days of the challenge."

"The other legislation was proposed by Sens. Lindsey Graham, R-S.C., and Cory Booker, D-N.J. It would prevent the firing of any special counsel unless the dismissal was first reviewed by a panel of three federal judges."

"Senators move to protect special counsel in Russia probe"; by Mary Clare Jalonick; Associated Press; August 3, 2017

https://www.yahoo.com/news/senators-move-protect-special-counsel-russia-probe-073325273--politics.html

August 2, 2017

Five bipartisan proposals for health care stabilization: (1) "mandatory funding of cost-sharing reduction payments"; (2) "move CSR allocations under the Congressional appropriations process to ensure greater oversight"; (3) "create a stability fund state governments can use to keep premiums at a reasonable level"; (4) "bumping the threshold for the employer health care mandate from businesses of 50 employees to businesses of 500 employees" and (5) "defining a 'full-time' employee as someone who works 40 hours a week instead of 30."

"Arizona representatives sponsor bipartisan health care stabilization proposal"; Aug 2, 2017

https://www.bizjournals.com/phoenix/news/2017/08/02/arizona-representatives-sponsor-health-plan.html

August 2, 2017

"Future Shock" - 21st Century (1) Recent high temperature mortalities associated with heatwaves have recently occurred in Chicago (~740 deaths, 1994), Paris (~4,870 deaths in 2003) and Moscow (~10,860 deaths in 2010). High heat is linked to deregulation of body temperature and high humidity is linked to reduced sweating i.e. both factors result in multiple organ failure: "Around 30% of world's population is currently exposed to climatic conditions exceeding this deadly threshold for at least 20 days a year. By 2100, this percentage is projected to increase to ~48% under a scenario of drastic reductions in greenhouse emissions and 74% under a scenario of growing emissions. An increasing threat to human life from excessive heat now seems almost inevitable, but will be greatly aggravated if greenhouse gases are not considerably reduced."

See - "Global risk of deadly heat"; Mora, C. et al; Nature Climate Change; 7: pgs 501-506

"Future Shock" 21st Century (2) Re: Sea Levels Rises (SLRs). A report entitled "Migration induced by sea-level could reshape the US population" by Matthew E. Hauer (Nature Climate Change,

May 2017, 7(5), pg 321) suggests that the adaptation cost of a 1.8 meter SLR by 2100 could eventually peak at ~ US1.1 trillion dollars/year. The extremes could include 2.5 million migrants out of Florida and 1.5 million emigrants into Texas. Questions in the Anderson Cooper/Al Gore include mitigation e.g. sea walls. However, even with mitigation, it is expected that 2 million Floridians will be forced to migrate. Climate change denial essentially leaves the adaptation cost of ~US1.1 trillion a "Future Shock" cost hidden by the Trump Administration's lack of foresight.

Made in the USA
Columbia, SC
01 November 2017